MARKETING CAMPAIGN
HANDBOOK

INSTRUCTIONS FOR OPERATING A SUCCESSFUL MARKETING CAMPAIGN

Volume 1

Bernice Loman, MBA

MARKETING CAMPAIGN
HANDBOOK

INSTRUCTIONS FOR OPERATING A SUCCESSFUL MARKETING CAMPAIGN

Volume 1

Bernice Loman, MBA

T&J PUBLISHERS

A SMALL INDEPENDENT PUBLISHER WITH A BIG VOICE

Printed in the United States of America by
T&J Publishers (Atlanta, GA.)
www.TandJPublishers.com

Cover design by Loman Creative Services
Book format and layout by Timothy Flemming, Jr.
(T&J Publishers)

ISBN: 978-1-7345105-5-3

To contact the author, go to:

www.lomancreativeservices.com
www.marketingcampaignhandbook.com

Contact Bernice at
bernice@marketingcampaignhandbook.com to leave reviews
and to acquire information about being a guest on the
Marketing Campaign Handbook Podcast for entrepreneurs.
#marketingcampaignhandbook.com

"Thanks to Loman Creative Services for assisting me in setting my church for more professional live-streaming. After purchasing and reviewing the webinar, I gained everything I needed. The webinar was so informative. I am thankful that Bernice Loman is a Christian Business and she understands the needs of the small church."

—Pastor Johnnie,
Restoration Worship Center

"I was amazed by Bernice Loman's professionalism, her quickness in getting work done, and her dedication to those she serves. She is a true gift to the business world."

—Timothy Flemming, Jr.,
Entrepreneur, Author, and Minister

This book is dedicated to God, my family, and friends.

A special thanks to Mr. Loman for pushing me to greater..

Big thanks for T&J Publishing and the Loman Creative Services team for all your help with making this possible.

TABLE OF CONTENTS

INTRODUCTION | WHY I WROTE THIS BOOK

THERE IS A GREAT NEED FOR THIS BOOK. I HAVE witnessed many entrepreneurs, business owners and ministry leaders who once proudly branded with a beautiful logo, banner, business cards, etc., and launched something yet struggled with getting their product or message to a particular audience. I created something that organizations can use as a guide - a step by step, on creating successful campaigns themselves and can help take them to another audience level. This book will definitely cut cost with hiring a marketing campaign firm initially as I give you the marketing campaign tools. While I do suggest hiring a marketing firm to help manage your campaigns as you grow, this book can be a tool to help you at least understand marketing campaigns and to point you in the right direction as you start.

MARKETING CAMPAIGN HANDBOOK

1 | WHAT IS BRANDING & MARKETING

- Branding vs. Marketing
- Creating a brand
- Creating brand materials

JUST IN CASE YOU HAVE A DIFFICULT TIME WITH differentiating the two-branding and marketing, I would like to first describe branding before elaborating on marketing and campaigns. Branding is identity. Your brand is who you are as an organization. There are different ways to identify your organization, it can be through culture, a logo, mission, design, and communication just to name a few. The branding culture is the substance of your organization. Know that you can have a logo and still not brand effectively because the culture has not been established. I suggest establishing a brand culture for your organization in the beginning. Brand culture is the DNA of your organization. The question to ask yourself is, what is your company's DNA? What is it made of? Scientifically, a DNA, deoxyribonucleic acid, can be used to tell people apart. Although there are many cells in a human body, nearly every cell in a person's body has the same DNA. Although your company may have different moving parts and competitors near, others should still be able to know your brand's DNA. What stands your brand apart? How would you like others, including your team members, to feel about your brand? How will everyone express themselves?

Each brand needs a tone. In the beginning of brand culture, you set the tone and style. How will every-one interact with your message? When you make the promise of quality products, services and de-livery, a corporate brand is established. How you attract potential custom-ers and communicate with your existing customers will identify your corpo-rate branding. Questions to ponder are, What type of re-sults would you like to aim

"Brand culture is the DNA of your organization. The question to ask yourself is, what is your company's DNA?"

for when creating your products or services? What is your organization's purpose? All this time you probably thought branding was just a logo. Well, at least most small business owners that I have con-sulted first thought so. The logo design and color is actually an easy process after culture has been established. I suggest gathering your organization team and have a discussion on the culture. Start with the questions that I have included.

There is such a thing as employer branding. This is when an employer or company leader focuses on educating the team so that they better understand the brand. I recommend having a quarterly team branding meeting. This is where you will discuss the vision, mission, goals, story, products and services-the company DNA. One of the key components to discuss with your team and audience is your story. I mean your brand story. A brand story is the emotions and facts that create your organization. An example would be sharing why you or the owner started the company, sharing your passion of connecting to the company, who you're called to serve and the why. Do you desire to build wealth? Do you have a passion to see others succeed? Who are you called to reach? All of these details matter and create your brand culture-DNA.

Once you have discovered your brand DNA, it's the time to CREATE! I highly recommend hiring a professional in your creating process. Remember, you are your brand. If you want to communicate quality, you must display quality. What you should be seeking is a skilled professional. Having a consultation is advised. Don't be afraid to ask for a portfolio and references. View some of their recent work. Graphic designers grow in time with experience and learn new skills. Now that you understand brand identity,

I recommend sharing your brand culture info with your graphic designer. Go to Google font website and view fonts. Communicate this to your graphic designer. Also discuss logo formats. The recommended logo formats are:

- .png
- .pdf
- .jpg
- .svg
- .eps
- .psd

If possible, ask for the logo editable file. Most logo designers design logos in Photoshop. It's an Adobe graphic design software.

The editable file is .PSD. Most graphic designers don't keep editable files for a long period of time because it takes up much space on the computer. Asking for your editable logo file in advance will save frustration later if you decide to change color or a slight design. I can't tell you how many times we've had new clients who asked us to make changes to their logo because they could no longer contact their former graphic designer nor have the editable file. Without an editable file, you would have to start completely over in designing a new logo. If you have not budgeted for a new logo design, this can be strenuous and inconvenient. The .png log file is a transparent file. I use this a lot with branding and marketing materials. Have you seen a logo with a white border? That isn't a .png, .svg, and .eps files are vector files that are perfect for t-shirts, billboards, banners, and anything that requires a blowout. The PDF file is good for printing such as letterheads, etc. As long as the jpeg is a 300 dpi, you should be fine with printing letterheads, business cards, flyers, etc.

Moving forward with printing material, I recommend branding packages. Begin with at least a logo design, website, business cards, rack cards, a letterhead, flyers, company shirts, and website and social media cover page designs. Brochures are not as popular as they once were. I've witnessed rack cards to be a fine substitution. Each material should have your company's logo, brand color and font. With your business cards, be personal. When you first establish your brand, I suggest adding your headshot on your business card. It puts a face to your brand and name. Please make sure that you have a professional headshot. Invest into your local professional photographer who can assist you and your team. If you have a team, each of them should use the same photographer so that the brand displays the same DNA. When I begin my marketing campaigns, I seek the company's photos. I first looked for three recent headshots. If you have not had a professional headshot taken within 1-2 years, it's time. The industry standard is every 1-2 years. If you have made a drastic change in your appearance in less than 1 year, you should consider getting a new headshot. It's imperative that your headshot represents you. This, too is a part of your brand. I remember a few times where I was a guest at a program and the speakers that I saw on the flyer didn't look anything like what I imagined. Ask yourself, is my brand image out-dated? Take a look at your website and marketing materials also to see if you have old photos. Later in my upcoming chapters, I'll discuss websites.

Perhaps you have been in business or ministry for quite some time and this language is foreign to you. Rebranding isn't abnormal. As your culture and message change, consider changing your brand identity. Well-known brands such as AT&T, Canon, Kodak, Shell, Apple, just to name a few, have changed their logo. You can too with confidence and no apology! Before I start my marketing campaigns, I also reflect back on the company's brand. It helps me drive an effective campaign. You don't drive a car without oil and gas. You shouldn't want to drive your products and services to an audience without a brand identity. Keep reading and you too can learn how to drive an effective marketing cam-

> "You don't drive a car without oil and gas. You shouldn't want to drive your products and services to an audience without a brand identity."

paign like a pro.

SNAPCHAT GEO FILTERS: ANOTHER WAY TO BRAND

If you are having an upcoming event, have a ministry or business, having a snapchat geofilter is the way to go! There are "more than 100 million active Snapchat users" so imagine how important it will be to have your name, logo or trademark exposed to over 100 million customers! It's even more fun at an event! Why not brand your event and have everyone log on Snapchat at your event, take a photo with YOUR FILTER (your brand) and share it with their friends! How cool is that?!!

If you target the right locations, your geofilter will interact with highly qualified potential customers — and everyone they know on Snapchat. For Geofilters, it's best to submit per day. So, if you have a two-day event, it's best to order for two days at once. The filter will last on Snapchat for 24 hours.

Facebook frames are another great way to brand.

WHAT IN THE WORLD IS BRANDING?
Creating a Personality Brand and a Corporate Brand - *It's like lions and tigers and bears, oh my*

Branding is a term you surely hear when starting a business. Different coaching and consulting agencies tell you to establish your brand, but what does it truly mean? Branding is the process of creating a set of "normals" for your business model or idea. Some items that you commonly think of when the word *branding* is mentioned are logos, letterhead, a website, colors and taglines. These are parts in the branding puzzle. You recognize big brands such as Facebook, Microsoft, and Apple. Getting your brand built won't start at their level, but will start at your level. Your website should contain all of the parts of your branding experience.

Understanding business means having a good, clear vision of your personality and corporate brand together as one flowing brand. You, after all, are your own brand, and thus, you need to be happy with the unity of your personality and corporate brand. Let's explore some of the options for branding and how they affect the success of your business now and in the future.

Personality Branding is that flow associated with who you are. For example, if you are what is called a "woo woo" you may prefer the pinks and purples in your personality brand. If you are strict, straight-lined, left-brained, you may want to keep your colors neutral or with a hint of business such as blue-gold, red-gold. Either way, you must have a brand that is cohesive with your likes and the goals of your business.

Getting comfortable with a "Personality Brand" means figuring out who you are and what makes you smile. You can consider things like what type of clothes you like to wear, what type of speaking personality you possess, and what type of things can you talk about to your prospects which will connect you to them at a deep level. Once you have established your personality brand, then you can branch outward into a corporate brand. Your corporate brand will have a unique life of its own but will tie back into your personality brand.

> "Understanding business means having a good, clear vision of your personality and corporate brand together as one flowing brand."

In deciding your corporate or business brand, consider the method you will connect your two brands. Let's say you are a jeans and t-shirt kind of lady, or man, your corporate brand could very well be blue and easy flowing, with handwritten type fonts. If your style is a business suit then you can go with straight fonts and simply colors for your lo-gos, graphics, and other elements of your business marketing strategy.

Remember you want a brand to be sticky. So, rather than jumping out into the marketplace with a brand you can't keep up with, or sacrificing your person-ality needs in order to build the brand "they" tell you to build, start from the beginning by knowing you will be happier if you can blend your brands. A good tip is to search Google for brands that speak to you. You can also be alert to brands that you don't like at all. Your website, business cards, logos, and asset needs should all match.

2 | WHAT IS A CAMPAIGN?

- Marketing Campaigns
- Communications
- Transitioning from branding to marketing
- Websites
- Email Campaigns

A CAMPAIGN IS *AN ORGANIZED EFFORT TO REACH a specific goal*. Three main things to consider in a campaign is the why, the specific goal, and how are you going to get there. Here is an example:

You need donations for your 501c3. Your *why* may be because you want to provide shelter for the homeless. During your "why," it's a great time to highlight your passion and story. If you have been homeless before and have a great need to give back, that is attached to your "why". The goal would be to provide clothing for 3,000 homeless men and women. In between the why and the goal is determining how will you reach your goal. How will you reach your goal? Start with setting realistic goals. I know we people of faith can believe God for everything but we at times fail to take action.

With campaigns, set realistic goals. If you only have three people on your team and none of them are computer savvy, you may want to decrease your goal if you expect to share your story through tech avenues. Setting realistic goals is wise. You can create several campaigns to split your efforts. If your large goal is to clothe 3,000 homeless men and women, you can create three campaigns and reach 1,000 homeless men and women for each campaign. My mom always told me, "there's more than one way to skin a cat". Be creative in your campaign efforts. Start each campaign by setting the why and the goal and discuss how will you reach your goal. There are several marketing channels to use to help you reach your goal with a successful marketing campaign. Let's first understand what marketing campaigns are.

UNDERSTANDING MARKETING CAMPAIGNS

Marketing campaigns promote services, products or a message through different types of media such as online platforms, radio, television, and print. Please understand that campaigns are not solely reliant on ads. With today's modern tools, you can use webinars, livestream, demonstrations, and other interactive techniques. An effective marketing campaign requires strategy, effort, consistency and awareness of the market. I'll later share some strategy tips that can help you with creating a successful marketing campaign.

When creating a marketing campaign, you definitely need a plan. Knowing what, when and how is very essential. WHAT is your message, product or service and what tool(s) will you use to get your message, product or service to the world? When will you create your campaigns and make it available to the world? How will it be managed? Being aware of the market is a plus. I can't count the numerous times I've witnessed an entrepreneur launch something and then later get hit with market competition and forever changing trends. I'll later share the importance of research. It's with strategy that you get a plan of action on when it's time to launch and how to maintain successfully in the market.

> Remember: Marketing is simply moving a message to the masses. To do this, you need an effective marketing campaign.

TRANSITIONING FROM BRANDING TO MARKETING

I personally believe that branding well makes the next step in marketing smooth. Once everyone on the team and audience understands who you are as an organization, the call to action is normal. See below the steps in transitioning from branding to marketing:

1. Branding with culture
2. Mission and vision
3. Communication (Your story)
4. Logo
5. Design (website, business cards, postcards, etc.)
6. Research
7. Target audience
8. Content marketing
9. Marketing strategy
10. PR plan
11. Media plan including social media

Exercises

BRANDING WITH CULTURE
Record a 15 seconds video of you describing your company. Later in this book, I'll discuss the importance of video.

MISSION AND VISION

Create or get a flyer created with your company's logo, contact info and mission and vision. You'll be amazed at one of the reasons why sales don't increase is because the company's mission and vision isn't clear. Everything you do should reflect your company's mission and vision.

COMMUNICATION

Write your story in 3 lines. Memorize it. This would be perfect for your elevation pitch. An elevation pitch is a persuasive quick synopsis of your background.

LOGO

View your existing logo. Form a meeting with your team or those who you trust and ask for their honest opinion of your logo. Do not use logos or trademarks that you don't own or have authorization to use. You can search trademarks at www.uspto.gov. This website is also where you go to trademark your logo. Go to the "Apply for a Trademark" tab. It would be dangerous to start a branding and marketing campaign to later get sued for copyright and trademark infringement. If you don't have a logo yet, that's okay too. You have invested in this book and it will help guide you on the next step in logo design and brand.

DESIGN

Evaluate all of your design packages and see if it matches your brand culture, mission and vision. Are the fonts the same on all designs? Are the colors the same? I recommend getting your brand's hex color. A website like https://htmlcolorcodes.com/color-picker/ will allow you to choose your hex colors. Having your hex colors will help tremendously when working with a graphic and/or designer also. Having hex colors in advance will help avoid a brand mis-communication. Try using your brand's hex colors with EVERYTHING - logo, flyers, business cards, rack cards, etc. Remember your brand DNA. As your company grows, you will notice different moving parts. Don't forget your brand, story and its mission.

RESEARCH

Marketing requires research! Marketing research is important in the target audience identification process. Marketing research is the process of collecting, analyzing and interpreting information about your target market, potential clients, competitors and the industry as a whole. There are several key holders in this process and that is why it takes time to collect data and analyze. I'll try my best to give you a step-by-step guide so that it's not foreign language. Do you have a new company? If so, you would need to research in your business area locally to see if there's a need for your brand, products and services.

Conducting a survey would be beneficial. Use survey platforms such as Survey Monkey. Survey Monkey is a free online survey tool that you can use to capture opinions. Ask potential customers what they like about a specific product or service that you plan to offer. Ask them if they are currently using this product. If they are currently using this product or service, ask them about the brand. What do they like about the brand? Price and time is a huge factor on surveys. This information is important. You need to know what are the majority willing to spend and where they spend most of their time. If the majority spends most of their time at the gym, you should consider your product or service that compliments workout activity. Now, ponder for a minute or two. What product or service do you have that can compliment the activity of your ideal client. If you're already an established business, this is still a good idea.

Write down at least 10 products or services that you have and match them with the activity of your client. If you aren't already, send out quarterly surveys. Google forms is another online survey tool. Each survey can be customized and survey results can be exported in a spreadsheet. This gives you an opportunity to analyze data that has been collected. Google forms are free with a personal Google account. With Google Suite, there's a small monthly fee but it includes security. I suggest Google Suite for any organization. Google Suite's business plan includes a Gmail business email, shared calendars, cloud storage, secure team messaging, video and voice conferencing, Word Docs, spreadsheets, presentation slides builder, and more!

Startups, when researching your industry, search globally as well. I previously included the government's trademark website information. You can also use that website as a great source. Doing a random Google search helps also. Search to see if the company name that you would like to use has already been branded. Search for symbols and see if the logo design that you imagined has already been used or trademarked. Research slogans if you prefer to have a slogan. Examples of well-known slogans are "Just Do It", "It's finger licking' good", I'm lovin' it", just to name a few. I'm often asked, "should I include my slogan in my logo design?" I personally believe that you should have the freedom to use your logo without your slogan if you like. If you decide to create another product and would like to add another slogan, removing the slogan from an original logo file can be time consuming. You have options and it's totally your preference.

One step I use to research words is Google alerts at www.google.com/alerts. I'm able to monitor the web for interesting new content. I add in keywords. When the words become available online, whether in a blog, on a website, a post, etc., Google will alert me. This is an excellent tool for research. We use and trust Google for almost everything right? Why not use it for web alerts? Well, I do! You can also research with surveys. Google forms www.google.com/forms or Survey Monkey www.surveymonkey.com are two good survey platforms that can be used to create a poll. Simply ask people what they want. I don't recommend launching any product, service, event, message, etc. without researching the market. Supply the demand. If there's no demand, don't supply. That's simple. Don't be guilty of creating something where there is no demand. Research the time also. Timing is everything. Ecclesiastes 3 states that there is a time for everything. Apply this principle to your campaign. It works!

KEEPING YOUR WEBSITE CURRENT TO KEEP YOUR LEADS COMING

Having a website, as you know, is the first step in a successful business. Buying a website, the design service, setting up wordpress and working on SEO goals cannot end when the design work is complete. In fact, keeping your website current is as important as building it to begin with. Your brand may change, your outlook may change, and certainly your product offering may change.

Most importantly, sometimes in website design, everything changes. We recommend you consider how and when you will update your WordPress, how often will you purge old content, and how often will you create brand new website copy. When you can see that your business changes quickly, you will feel eager to keep your website current. Knowing which plugins to use, how to word your sales copy so people buy your product and keeping a current email marketing funnel active all require maintenance.

When you have a high-quality website on Word-Press, hosted with a professional hosting service, you have lots of options for keeping current. The plugins need to be updated so they continue to work with the current version of your WordPress install. WordPress.org itself needs to be updated periodically, and a quality check on the success of your optimization platform needs to be conducted to ensure your website is doing what it needs to do. Your ultimate goal is for the website to sell products on its own, right?

THE IMPORTANCE OF SELLING ONLINE

You must sell online to survive in business. We cannot stress enough the importance – online selling – is to the success of your business. Almost every industry has been affected by the onslaught of online sales. From books to automobiles, if there is something that can be sold, it can be purchased online. The ease of setting up an online storefront may not be noticeable at first, but with the proper guidance, you can have your own storefront up and running in no time.

Whether you are selling products or services, you must know how to be a salesman, or saleswoman in order for your business to stay afloat. If you are selling services, for example, you surely need to have your website and marketing system in place. When you have a well-oiled machine to send your prospects through, selling becomes easier. Here are three important ways to sell your services

"You must sell online to survive in business."

easier:

1. Having a great social media outreach across all social media networks. When your message is clear, quite often a service is sold before a phone consultation ever takes place. Of course, you want your WordPress website to integrate with your social media profile.

2. Website Copy (or the text on your website) is also a great way to mitigate objections, create a situation of easy selling and convince your website visitors to ACT! Meaning, you want them to click a link and follow through.

3. Visualize closing the sale, well before you have sold it to a person. Visualization is one of the most important techniques in selling. The more confident you are in closing a deal, the more yeses you will get and the better you will feel.

Online selling is not hard. You must develop the backbone for it, get out there and put your greatness to the world, and believe that your product, service or promotion is valuable to your prospects. There are millions of men and women who shop online every day. You should have your products out there for them to see.

2 WHAT IS A CAMPAIGN?

SEARCH ENGINE OPTIMIZATION (SEO)

Past, Present and Future Trends for gaining momentum, lead attraction and visibility on search engines.

If you are in business or are considering going into business locally with a store or virtually with an online business, you will be confronted with the term SEO. I have seen people who use these 3 letters as a noun, verb and adjective. The truth is that SEO is defined as Search Engine Optimization. As you may suspect, it is to increase your visibility in searches on search engines such as Google, Bing and Facebook. To maximize your time, it's important that you are aware of where this term originated, the method by which current searches are indexed and trends coming in the future.

We will start with Google, the world's largest search engine. Google is a highly intuitive indexing software that feeds results to the user based on the data typed into the search box. Google started out with just a few websites in a program that indexed those websites and fed them as a result for the searcher. In the past, keywords that were specific to the search results were the main source of information needed for the software to generate the best possible link for the "words" entered.

In the past, web developers would make their copy heavy with keywords, which became obviously overwhelming to the searcher because you would ultimately come across a page with 100s of repeated words. This was not functional for many reasons, the first being the discomfort of reading such single word heavy pages.

Fast forward to present. Google has improved its intuitive algorithm to include sentences, authentic and organic content, searching or "mining" a plethora of databases of websites, blogs, social media posts and press exposure to feed to the searcher ALL of the results that fit the search terms entered. While Google is certainly not the only search engine, it is the basis by which all others work so we will continue with Google SEO. Google expanded its indexing and results driven method, to move away from a number system such 1. The best result 2. A variety of the best results, etc. to facilitate a more natural results generation. This change also started to usher in voice commanded search results.

Another current method that Google has built on in recent years is voice activated mobile searches. By speaking into your phone and saying "Ok Google" you can ask very specific questions and expect very specific results. For example: "Ok Google (bleep), How do I get back home?" Enter – responsive technology based on where you are at the current time, what you have indicated as being home, and how long it will take you to arrive at your destination called home.

With this voice string, Google pulls up a map, starts the navigator and tells you were to turn next. It is really amazing what Google does every day. So, where is all of this going in the future?

You can expect Search Engine Optimization to improve based on the needs of people doing the searching. Google has expanded into the home with its revolutionary "Google Home" where you can ask it things from across the room, instruct it to turn lights on and off and get the current whether without the need for a computer or phone.

To ensure you are fully optimizing your Search Engine Optimization, keep a blended content base across a wide - spectrum of databases. Keep a blog going with lots of unique posts to get visitors to your website. Keep your social media posts in line with your blog and post your blogs all across your social media. Be guests on talk shows and podcasts to get results related to published media. *Get SEO at www.lomancs.biz*

PRIVATE DOMAIN

How much is privacy worth to you? Did you know that anytime you register a domain, your personal information is exposed 24 hours a day? Your name, Your address, Your phone number, Your email. It is all published online for anyone to see, as mandated by ICANN. But you have the power to change this. With Private Registration:

- Your domain is registered under the name Domains by Proxy, so its information is made public — not yours.
- You retain full control of your domain. You can cancel, sell, re-new or transfer your domain, set up name servers for your domain and resolve disputes involving your domain.
- You manage and control all email addressed to the domain, as well as the domain's contact information, with Domains by Proxy's patented registration and email handling systems.
- You are still accountable for your actions. Don't even think about using a private registration to transmit spam, violate the law or engage in morally objectionable activities.

PROFESSIONAL EMAIL

- Create a unique and professional email address based on your domain.
- Build your business identity
- Put your company name in front of customers and prospects, suppliers, vendors and partners with every email you send.

2 WHAT IS A CAMPAIGN?

- Receive only the email you want
- We stop spam in its tracks to keep your inbox squeaky clean.
- Get live, expert help
- Our U.S.- based customer care consultants, available 24/7/365.
- Grab your email anywhere, including from your Web browser, mobile phone, tablet and desktop clients like Outlook or Mac Mail.

3 | CONTENT MARKETING

- Benefits of Content Marketing
- Ways to distribute content
- Livestream Marketing

ONTENT IS SIMPLY INFORMATION. MARKETING IS impossible without good content. Content marketing is creating and distributing valuable information to drive interaction. With your goal in mind, create and distribute information that matches where you're going and your mission and vision. Your goal may be to capture 50 more leads. By the way, a lead is a person who may eventually become a client. If your goal is to capture 50 more leads, you should create content on your product or services and create a landing's page

A landing page is a one page website that will allow web visitors to add their information (name, email, etc.) and receive information or purchase a product/ service. I suggest you become creative with your landing page by adding an intro video. Videos help your audience absorb information better and to become more engaging. For your video, you should add the top 5 benefits of your product/service and then add a call-to-action.

For ministries who may not have a product, know that you are packaging the Gospel, love, peace, etc. You are promoting salvation, and a better living. For your landing page video, you should list the top 5 reasons to stay connected to God and highlight great things about your ministry. In the later chapter "The Marketing Plan," I share the call-to-action more in-depth.

> "Content is simply information. Marketing is impossible without good content."

Here are benefits of content marketing:

- Increases brand visibility
- Develops lasting relationships with your existing customers
- Improves brand awareness
- Creates loyalty and trust
- Helps you to build credibility
- Positions your organization as an expert in your industry

Exercise
List 5 benefits of your product/service

1. _____

   _____

2. _____

   _____

3. _____

   _____

4. _____

   _____

5. _____

   _____

With content marketing, you should plan, produce, promote and analyze. With the 5 benefits that
you listed above, you can include in your market-

ing campaign. In fact, I suggest highlighting each of your strengths in your campaign. Take each of those benefits and create a blog, webinar and Facebook live. An online course would be great too! For example, one of the benefits of using our social media management services is that an organization has more time to work on their business while Loman Creative Services handles the postings, engagement, videos, graphics and more. With that just one benefit, we created a social media webinar Don't forget your brand DNA. Remember your brand as you are creating and distributing. Previously, I shared an example of a 501c3. An example of content marketing for that non-profit would be sharing the top reasons why men become homeless. You can create data of how many single mothers are homeless. Research and content marketing are siblings. Good research creates an outstanding content marketing campaign.

WAYS TO DISTRIBUTE CONTENT

These are several ways to distribute content:

- Blogging
- Video
- Podcasting
- Infographics
- Email
- Ebooks/Books

- Slideshare presentations
- Quizzes
- Courses
- Webinars
- Social media posts

I know the list is long. Let me give you a strategy on how to tackle these above. First, write down at least a key subject. Share what you will be discussing. Having a key subject will help you stay focused on the point you want to make. Then write down at least three points around the subject. Add statistics, other experts' opinions or quotes and your expertise. Record a 30 minute to 1 hour video to discuss this subject and key points. Add your brand story. Let me add, in my opinion, Iphones have an excellent video quality. I still love my Android user friends. Don't worry. (I'm laughing). I recommend that you eventually invest in a DSLR camera. DSLR stands for Digital Single Lens Reflex. These are professional cameras that capture well and are great for Youtubers, bloggers, etc. I have DSLR cameras that I recommend at my website www.lomancreativeservices.com/tech-products.

I suggest that you record a 30 minute to 1 hour video and transcribe the video into text. An application called Trint is a good source. Visit https://app.trint.com/signup. You can take your text content and then post on your blog posts, infographics, ebooks/books, email, social media posts, etc. Create courses and webinars from your text also. Add the text to presentation slides so that you can use it for your webinars. I like to add text to my graphic. You may not be a graphic artist to use Adobe Suite (Illustrator, Photoshop, InDesign, etc.) but you can use Canva to help you brand and share your content. Anchor.fm is a good source for free podcasting. It is totally free and they distribute to major podcast platforms like Apple Itunes, Google Podcast, Spotify, etc. Submit your podcast to Trint and have content for your blog, website, social media posts, and more. Create a Periscope/Twitter account if you don't have one. Periscope allows live audio. It is another creative way to share content. It is not difficult to share content. All you need to do is utilize technology and strategize. In the earlier chapters, I shared how you can find your target audience. By now, you should know who your target audience is and where they are located from conducting a survey, market researching and a SWOT analysis.

FLYERS

Flyers are another good way to share content. Flyers are a useful tool to help build awareness about your brand. If you have a political campaign, printed flyers are most essential because it leaves a personal touch impression. People are visual and love tangible things. If your goal is to reach 10,000 people, I suggest printing out that number of flyers with a QR code that directs people to your website. A QR Code is a two-dimensional version of a barcode.

It's a quick way where people can scan from their phone to get to your website or any website url you choose. They are created with a QR code generator. Visit www.qr-code-generator.com to create one. With today's technology, digital flyers have become more popular. I recommend that you create digital flyers to share across your digital platforms: text, website, social media, and so on). Boosting a flyer on social media can get just as much of an effect as posting tons of flyers. While there are people who love tangible flyers, there are some who prefer digital. Keep that in mind when planning for your marketing campaign.

TEXT MARKETING

You can also use text marketing to share your digital flyers. Text marketing will allow others to join your text list through text and get feed with your content through their mobile phone. There are now land-line text services as well. However, I suggest the mobile phone option. With text marketing, you can create a compelling call-to-action, pick the right cadence, make offers exclusive and personalize text messages. I use EZ Texting. www.eztexting.com Their prices are affordable for a small business. However, there are plenty more companies out there so research which is better for your budget and needs. The strategy that I use is I send out three communications, email, social media and text. Be sure to stay in front of your leads and customers' eyes. You provide a solution and they should know.

VIDEOGRAPHY

Many of you (including myself) have been encouraged by Bishop Jakes, Pastor Joel Osteen, Joyce Myers, John Maxwell, Dr. Winston, Bill Gates videos, just to name a few. Although we are not physically there with them, their videos have impacted us. Imagine the many lives you can empower with a video? Videography is powerful! I highly recommend it for your small business, ministry and especially a larger corporation. There are many ways to use videos, just to name a few:

- DVDs
- Digital Download
- Youtube Channel
- IGTV
- Facebook, Instagram and Snapchat Story
- Livestream
- Website Tutorials or Introductions
- Online Classes
- Webinars

Again, just to name a few. There are other creative ways to use videos and to increase income for you and your team. Let me share with you that, the attention span is 8 seconds according to The New York Times. Why not capture attention with an eye-catchy and professional video. If you don't have a budget for a DSLR camera, use your smartphone with good lighting. Amazon has LED lights for under $60. Invest in two so that you have one on both sides of you but in front of you. Your light should always be in front of you. Invest in a lapel microphone so that your audio sounds good. I have my lapel mic recommendations at my website www.lomancreativeservices.com. It's important that when marketing, quality is chosen. When you have quality products and services, it's not hard to market it. Others can easily see the value in a product or service when the images and videos are good.

Consider investing into television commercials. Due to social media, tv commercials aren't as cost effective but there's still an audience that still enjoy watching tv. If you have the budget, I recommend investing in tv commercials. TV commercials are advertising.

According to the Small Business Chronicle, here are the Advantages of Television Advertising:

- Grabs attention
- Combines sight and sound
- Fosters emotion and empathy
- Reaches a wide, targeted audience
- It's a big production
- Frequency is essential

Marketing is preparing a product for the marketplace. Advertising is making your product and service known to the marketplace. Advertising is a component of marketing. Advertising uses the data that is collected from marketing strategies to better communicate the brand.

Forms of advertising are newspapers, magazines, direct mail, billboards, tv, radio and online. Facebook, Instagram and LinkedIn boosted ads are popular online. I later discuss budgeting and will discuss budgeting tips for ads. Advertising can be costly and is the biggest cost in marketing.

> "Marketing is preparing a product for the marketplace. Advertising is making your product and service known to the marketplace.."

MARKETING WITH A LIVESTREAM STRATEGY

By now, you should see the need for livestream especially from a recent pandemic. Millions, including churches, utilized livestream to stay connected. It is imperative to have a live video strategy so that your organization won't be another live video just like the rest. A live video strategy engages viewers. Say this with me: authenticity and engagement. That is the KEY! What makes a livestream stand out most is the authenticity and engagement. st in immediate and authentic ways that other social media formats cannot. Marketers understand the value of livestream and invest in livestream by purchasing ads.

Most people enjoy watching a live show that's behind-the-scenes. Take notice, even very few tv shows are edited anymore. There are more live tv shows. We humans enjoy authenticity and a good subject that we can relate to. Having a subject that your target audience can relate to will produce engagement. Live Streaming is a good tool to use when marketing. I suggest before going live, set a topic, date and time. Create a reminder graphic so others who follow can be alarmed when you go live. For livestream, you can use your Facebook, Youtube, Instagram or Periscope/Twitter application. Remember, people enjoy authenticity. When going live and/or recording pre-recorded videos, share the behind the scenes.

For example, if you have an event coming up, share a video of you talking to the event coordinator, going to the store to pick up items for the event, or you going to the post office to pick up mail for the event. That is called story building. That is why Insta-story and Facebook stories are so popular. They are mini snaps, like Snapchat, of behind the scenes. If you haven't already, begin using Insta-story and Facebook stories every day. Record a 15 seconds video clip at least twice a week to share with your audience. If you would like to add graphics, lower-thirds and more, I recommend using a streaming software OBS Studio. It's a free open source software that's compatible for both PC and Mac. If you need any training, schedule at my website.

4 | THE MARKETING PLAN

- Target Market
- A Positioning Statement
- Value
- Goals
- Pricing
- SWOT Analysis
- Budget and Planning

THESE BOOK CHAPTERS ARE YOUR MARKETING PLAN guide. In each chapter, you can learn what each step of a marketing plan is and how to implement it. In the earlier chapter, you learned ways to identify your target audience. When identifying your target audience, A positioning statement is an expression of how a given product, service or brand fills a particular consumer need in a way that its competitors don't.

Here is the format of a positioning statement:
1. Target - Who is your product, services, or brand for.
2. Brand - Title your brand's name. This is where you will add your company, products, or ser-

vice's name.

3. Category - What area will your brand be competing in.
4. Key Benefit - Include the end benefits.
5. Differentiator - Include what stands you apart. Knowing what stands you apart from the rest of the industry and competitors can help tremendously with marketing campaigns.

Here's Loman Creative Service's positioning statement as an example:

"Since 2011, Loman Creative Services has been on a mission to make businesses and ministries more visible off and online with it's one-stop shop services ranging from Tv and radio ads, social media marketing, website development, graphic design, and technology training just to name a few. Today, serving thousands of clients globally, and building international partnerships such as Google, GoDaddy, Zoom and more, Loman Creative Services continues to strive to be one of the world's top marketing firms. Loman Creative Services gives organizations the tools they need to create a successful marketing campaign and online brand."

Now that you've seen my positioning statement for my business, it's time to create yours:

_____

_____

_____

_____

_____

_____

_____

_____

_____

_____

_____

_____

VALUE

Know what value you offer. This will differentiate you from the rest in your industry. Earlier, I asked you to list 5 benefits of your services/products. That is a great start. Added value can cause repeat business and brand loyalty.

TARGET AUDIENCE

Earlier, you learned how to identify your target audience. Often, your analysis will include specific factors like age, income, location and so on. This data is needed when marketing and advertising. When you study your target audience factors, you can effectively place your brand before their eyes. If your target audience is 50 and over, you might not want to market on Snapchat. You should consider television and Facebook. If your target audience are all professionals, you should consider Linkedin. If your target audience are women who shop, you should be on Pinterest. Those are some examples. Remember, I earlier mentioned the importance of surveys. Collecting survey data can help you in the target audience process.

You can use research by defining your target audience. Some ways to define your target market are:

4 THE MARKETING PLAN

1. Looking at your current customer base, knowing who they are and why do they purchase from you. Having a way to track your purchase data is a plus. I recommend you track your best seller product and which customers order that particular product. Where are your customers located? Hubspot is a good resource. It is a full platform of marketing, sales, customer service and a CRM software. www.hubspot.com. With Hubspot, you can organize, track and develop relationships with leads and customers. A CRM is a Customer Relationship Management system. It helps to manage customer data. This process is highly important in marketing because you need to know who you are marketing to.

2. Analyze your product and/or services. There's such a thing in conducting a competitive product analysis. How do your products and services compare to your competitor? I know, I know, you may not want to discuss competition and view it as a threat. The average business owner that I consult with is optimistic and wants to focus on his and her business. Knowing that someone's product may be 50% less than yours can have a major impact on your business. Knowing the market matters. I suggest creating a SWOT Analysis. A SWOT stands for Strengths, Weaknesses, Opportunities, and Threats. Strengths and weaknesses are internal to your company. These things you have control over.

3. Opportunities and threats are external to your company and you don't have control over. I suggest making adjustments to improve your strengths and weaknesses. Through findings in a SWOT, you can effectively move forward in the marketplace and quickly capitalize on opportunities. This makes marketing easier. Don't be alarmed, you may discover in your SWOT findings that it may not be the right time to move forward in business yet. Waiting is fine too. You want to make sure that when you launch, there is a high demand for your products and/or services, you're able to sustain the growth and still exist for decades. If you have an established business or ministry, a SWOT Analysis is recommended every six months. If you haven't scheduled a SWOT Analysis meeting with your team this year, it's a perfect time now to pause on reading this book and set a date now. Literally, pause NOW and set a date for your next SWOT Analysis meeting. A SWOT Analysis helps to build a positive reputation. Building a solid reputation can increase sales. Don't launch another product or service without a SWOT.

GATHERING A TEAM

Forming a marketing campaign requires hard work. I highly recommend having a team that can help manage the workload. You need a team that...

- can help REBRAND YOUR LOGO and WEBSITE
- who is responsible for the RESTRUCTURE OF THE MEDIA TEAM
- who can CREATE AN ONLINE STRATEGY
- who can manage your social media and IN-CREASE YOUTUBE SUBSCRIBERS
- and who can EXPAND EMAIL LISTS

There are other responsibilities, but I suggest starting with these to help guide you in the early stage of your marketing campaign.

COUNTING THE COST
(Budgeting)

As I stated before, Advertising can be costly and is the biggest cost in marketing. Setting a budget is IMPORTANT. For a small organization (less than 50 people), I recommend setting a monthly budget of $1,200. For organizations between 51-150, I suggest setting a budget of $2,400. The more people you have on the team, the marketing budget should increase because more people can produce value in results of sales. More sales equal more funding. More funding equals a larger budget. I suggest creating a marketing campaign for 6 months. Most tv ads start at $1200/month. Most radio ads start at $1100. Most tv and radio firms require a 6 months campaign, that cost can be close to $8,000. For an average small business/ministry, it's a high cost.

This leads most smaller organizations to only rely on social media and word of mouth. With much online competition, many brands are suffering on social media. There is a great need to stand apart. I suggest begin marketing well on social media and through email marketing first and then transitioning to advertisement once the clientele is built from online marketing. You know what you can afford.

MEDIA PLAN INCLUDING SOCIAL MEDIA

We cannot talk about marketing today without discussing the importance of social media marketing to your overall marketing strategy. There are many benefits to having a strong social media strategy, but the #1 benefit is the low cost of this platform. I am sure you use Facebook, probably every day. Even more so, probably more than once per day, every day of the week. If you, a prospective consumer, are on Facebook, Twitter, LinkedIn, Pinterest and a plethora of other social network sites, then you can now start to see how to use this low - cost marketing outlet for your own organization.

Social media is simply a term that has been coined over the last 10 years to mean a gathering of people on a website through chats, posts, shares and likes. Facebook has over 1.6 billion registered users and many registered and active users report using Facebook first thing in the morning. With this data at your fingertips, you can now start to apply the lessons in previous chapters to your overall marketing strategy.

You may be asking, how can I build brand awareness with social media? Your personality brand, as discussed previously, represents who you are inside. It is a natural base for the expansion of your corporate brand so let's start with your persona as others see it so you can create a winning social strategy right now. The way people see you is the way they see you for a long time, so make it right.

1. It's always a good idea to make your profile picture across social networks, look professional but look like your personal brand. It's a bad idea to have a picture of your pet or no profile picture at all. When you begin to market your business, your prospects are going to check you out left and right. So, have a good smile, and a clear picture for your profile picture.

2. Keep your message consistent across the social platforms, but don't over post. It's so easy to overdo it when posting to social media, and this may or may not be true, but keeping your message consistent across all platforms is key. If your message, for example, is on domestic violence awareness and a blog you have just started, you want to focus 90% of your time with marketing that is low-key but marketing still. If you offer a coaching service for $5000

and you are wanting to attract leads and close them on a contract, then you focus your message squarely on "why" your market needs your service, creating 4 posts of value and 1 post of sales.

3. Try very hard to keep your personal thoughts on politics and controversial items to a minimum, although we understand this is not easy to do. You want to maximize your marketing so that you attract paying clients who want to get you. If you are going on about your disappointment in the world around you, you may attract only persons who are disappointed in the world. Map your positive course and walk toward it every day in grace.

BECOMING FAMILIAR WITH THE SOCIAL MEDIA PLATFORMS

Become familiar with the several social media platforms. Even if you don't create an account for each of them, at least learn their purpose. I'm often asked, "which platform should I be on?" For any business, I at least recommend Facebook, Instagram, Youtube and LinkedIn. Each platform has different audiences and algorithms.

According to Sprout Social 2020...

- 51% of 13–17 year olds use Facebook.
- 76% of 18–24 year olds use Facebook.

4 THE MARKETING PLAN

- 84% of 25–30 year olds use Facebook.
- 79% of 30–49 year olds use Facebook.
- 68% of 50–64 year olds use Facebook.
- 46% of 65+ year olds use Facebook

If you would like to reach more of a younger audience, Instagram would be a better choice. Before I start my marketing campaign, I research where my target audience will be. This will help eliminate wasted time in graphics, videos, etc.

According to WebFX, here are 6 Best Social Media Platforms for Businesses:

1. Facebook - Number of monthly users: 2+ billion
2. Twitter -. Number of monthly users: 330 million
3. Instagram - Number of monthly users: 1+ billion
4. Pinterest - Number of monthly users: 300 million
5. LinkedIn - Number of monthly users: 303 million
6. YouTube - Number of monthly users: 2 billion

Social Media is practically a free marketing resource. You need the graphic collateral and sample posts to get started so – get started. Map out how you will fashion your posts, write a few samples and create a strategy.

THE PURPOSE OF A WEBSITE

Here's a few things that you will need for your website:

- SSL Certificate
- Website hosting
- Domain name
- Professional photos

When marketing, having an easy on the eyes website that web viewers can go to is best.

THE IMPORTANCE OF AN SSL CERTIFICATE FOR BUSINESS WEBSITES

Security is not a new term but is one that we must now begin to really take seriously. For business owners with websites, having information that comes in and goes out – being protected is key to long term business success and to avoiding crashes and hacking, or release of critical information. Showing your customers that your site is secure can be visualized by the graphic below.

What is an SSL Certificate? An SSL certificate serves as an electronic "passport." It establishes the website's authenticity and credibility and enables the browser and Web server to build a secure, encrypted connection. Without an SSL Certificate in place, your website information may be subjected to information leakage, cyber attack or hacking.

Credibility is established by checking the digital certificate, which includes:

- The Certificate holder's name (individual or company)
- The Certificate's serial number and expiration date
- A copy of the Certificate holder's "public" cryptographic key
- The digital signature of the Certificate-issuing authority

Extended SSL Certificates give the site visitor an additional visual cue, displaying the Certificate holder's name against a distinctive green background in the visitor's

What does an SSL protect from when generally used? For websites using Payment processing features, an SSL will help to prevent any private or personal information from leaking to other computers. It also encrypts all information coming in and going out. It's just a much safer choice than not choosing to add an SSL certificate to your website hosting package.

Your website is the home of your brand. It's where people go to learn more about you. They need to feel secure, safe and aware of the solution that you provide. Make sure that your home (website) is easy to navigate. Your website should be mobile-friendly and user-friendly. They should see your brand colors. Don't forget to include your font(s).

Here's a few safe website fonts:

- Arial - Arial is standard for most websites.
- Roboto
- Times New Roman
- Times
- Courier New
- Courier
- Verdana
- Georgia

If you are new to this concept or would like more information, visit www.lomancreativeservices.com

STREAMLINING TIME FOR BUSY ENTREPRENEURS

Are you a busy entrepreneur and find that you take on more tasks, run out of time, miss appointments and lose clients because your business needs help maximizing time? You are not alone. There are many ways to start improving the task of managing and monetizing time. Certainly, this is one of the major undertakings of a successful business.

There are only 24 hours in 1 day and some of the time you have to sleep.

Entrepreneurs and small business owners start out eagerly with anticipation of doing everything. One of the first business skills that falls by the wayside is time-management. Let's explore some ways a small business owner or eager entrepreneur can begin to improve and maximize the hours in a day.

First, learn quickly how to calendar and to remind yourself of appointments. Having notifications going off across your devices reminds you of appointments. While taking phone calls and having phone time are two of the main areas in business, there are other tasks that involve time. For setting appointments, make sure you give yourself a 30 minute cushion before and after phone calls so you can create a good phone strategy. Create your appointments based on importance. For example, you may want to allot an hour to someone whom you are trying to close on your big ticket item, while allowing phone calls for conversational purposes to go only 15 minutes or so.

Secondly, if you are in the service business, keep a close eye on the time you spend chatting on social media including answer messages unrelated to income generation for your business. Time-management for business is very important to the bottom line. If someone pops in on your messaging program and asks questions that are pertaining to the work you do, stop and take 2 minutes or more before you respond. The reason is that valuable business information can be given away for free during this type of time consuming exchange. Learn how to engage, offer and close a conversation on social media that impedes upon your time.

Finally, remember to schedule time for your self-care. Without you, there is no business. Running a small business can be overwhelming to your spirit and your health. Stop every day for at least 30 minutes and just be with yourself in prayer and silence. This is so good for you and the success of your business.

Indeed, time-management is one of the most important skills needed in a business. There are many websites that offer tools to streamline your time. Check them out. Maybe one or more of them are right for your business needs. Time is money.

Get a digital calendar at www.lomancs.biz

4 THE MARKETING PLAN

BUSINESS EXPANSION FOR ENTREPRENEURS AND SMALL BUSINESS

It's time to Expand. *Now what?* When we ask you what your plans are for business expansion, what answers come to mind? In today's busy economy, small or micro businesses often find the need to expand, happening rather quickly in the business cycle. Expanding can mean many things from moving out of the dining room office, into an actual office space. Or, it can mean adding a satellite office to your already successful business.

Expanding your business is something that should be in your current business model, even if the exact plan of expansion is not yet known. The point is that if you have a business, you want it to grow. Isn't this right?

There are a few things you must ask yourself when thinking about expanding your business:

1. What are the financial costs associated with expansion? When you decide what the financial costs are, you will have a better footing in deciding what type of expansion is needed. However, if the financial situation is grim, then you may want to reconsider the expansion. All expansion has an equal cost associated with it. A clear review of where your business is and where it wants to go, will assist you

with this question.

2. What are the immediate benefits of expansion, vs. the potential cost or loss associated with not expanding? You may see immediate benefits such as a better location generating more walk-in clients or having peace of mind when a virtual assistant is handling many tasks for you through outsourcing. In attempting to convince yourself "not" to expand you will want to explore the potential costs of not expanding. Get clear on your whys.

3. What personal changes will I need to make if the expansion progresses? While this may sound like a bizarre question, it is relevant. If you are accustomed to staying home with your baby all day, for example, expanding and going to an office every day may be harder than it seems. If you expand out and hire help, you will be stretched in ensuring they get the best training. Asking yourself what personal challenges will arrive is just smart care.

Most young businesses start out in their living room or garage. Just look at Apple and Microsoft. Both companies started in a garage. Expansion had to occur. Expansion happened and it happened quickly. In this changing market, the needs of your target market are also changing. Be there for the expansion when the time arises.

4 THE MARKETING PLAN

Here are 5 ideas for expanding your "online-only" business. These 5 tips will assist you in deciding on or waiting on expansion:

1. Go to Our Online Store and see that you can build an online store for as low as $25/month.
2. Create a new website and buy a new domain for the purpose of testing the market for your expansion.
3. Hit "Shark Tank" and apply to be on the show. You never know when your idea is the best one ever.
4. Consider using Email Marketing to grow clientele and keep your customers inform of sales
5. Create an idea map of programs, products, or services you can develop, or change so they can create cash flow for your business.

Deciding to expand is a natural and perfectly accepted need among business owners. You must expand to continue to grow, just choose carefully, when this expansion will occur.

THE GREATEST BENEFITS OF EMAIL MARKETING

Don't stop or stall your email marketing campaign just because you don't get fast results. It is so important that you understand the basics of email marketing and why the top online businesses have a high impact marketing campaign in all they do. One of the best ways you can see the power of email marketing is to open your own email and pick the one email that stands out to you. The company that sends out the email to you, is marketing the correct way. They are reaching you, you are opening your email, and you enjoy receiving the email. You may encounter doubts and create a million reasons to stop, stall or otherwise ignore email marketing. Contact me at info@lomancreativeservices.com and ask for the free trial of email marketing.

Social media has replaced email marketing for many businesses, but those businesses who stay afloat and thrive, keep up with their customers via email. If you are planning on opening a storefront online, email marketing is important because you can keep up with your clients via email, giving them customer specific sales and specials. If you are a coach, for example, and you run a service business, having an email campaign that gives a steady stream of inspiration to your prospects, can lead them to hire you to coach them.

Email marketing allows you to create and build up what is called a "Sales Funnel". The funnel is where you divert your prospects and leads. If you have a sales page for a website then you focus the words, graphics and action options toward selling your product. Then, if you don't close a sale, your prospects still are asked in several manners, to sign up to receive updates from you. This is called "Opting In" and they are then inside of your funnel. From inside of your funnel, they are able to receive hand-crafted messages from you, in their email in-box.

The more emails that go out and are read, the more likely your business is to convert the email to a close or a sale. The email messages will be written in a way to convince the prospect to take action. I have seen many successful email campaigns that make clicking, irresistible. Many professionals still rely only on email to get information and are slower to embrace social media as a way of marketing. So, to understand your business, understand that email marketing must be written into the flow of your business model from the beginning for your business to reap the benefits of a successful email campaign.

SALES IS A NECESSITY, NOT A FRINGE BENEFIT

When you are starting a business or are building an already established business, sales are simply a necessity and not a fringe benefit. In this post we are going to talk about some tools that can help you track your sales quickly and monitor them easily. With every business aspect there are good and bad situations. For example, while you want to keep up with the sales you make by selling products, programs, or services, you also want to mitigate chargebacks and refunds, and analyze setbacks and business killers.

We offer to you here, 3 simple strategies for maximizing the process of sales in your company, small or large. Follow these instructions for understanding business, and you will reap instant rewards:

1. What products, services, programs, or benefits do you provide in exchange for money? To sell a product you must have one to sell. Developing your product line up will require some work on your part but it will be worth it in the end. Create a basic MS Excel spreadsheet with your product names, product id., sales price, discounts (if any) and lifecycle. The clearer you can be on what products you sell, how much they will cost the consumer and your profit on sale, the easier you will make it from January to December with a positive outlook.

2. What payment processor will you use to collect money? Paypal is the obvious choice for many entrepreneurs who collect money online, but Paypal has a processing fee. Try it out and see if Paypal provides everything your business needs. Square is another company that processes online payments and offers hardware (a swiper) for you to collect credit and debit card payments at local events.

There is one major downfall with Square in that you cannot create payment or donation buttons as you can with Paypal.

3. Maximize your Facebook so you can close sales right from your Facebook page. Many of Facebook's new offerings are still in beta testing but for the most part, provide a method of selling right from a Facebook page. Using this method gives your business layers of options for sales. Sales are the "Life Blood" of your business so enlist and delegate if it is feasible and within your budget.

Tony Robbins, motivational speaker, says that a good sales representative will have compassion, a pleasant personality, and the ability to use ego-level energy to get the *yes* in the face of the *no's*.

WORDPRESS.COM VS. WORDPRESS ON A HOST

What is the different in WordPress.com and a Hosted WordPress Blog? WordPress is a blog-based platform that has evolved over the years. The ability to add quality content in many formats is one of the high points of having WordPress but many people get confused about what the difference is between WordPress.com and a blog hosted on a third- party server. We will look at the difference so you have a good understanding of which one to choose for your business.

First of all WordPress.com starts out free, and limited in the ability to customize the base template or "Theme". The theme forms the shell or skin of your website. This limitation may bother you as an entrepreneur because of its limited ability to alter the elements. Contrary to the limitations of a Wordrpess.com site, when you buy hosting and a domain name, then install the WordPress software you have plenty of creative options with your blog. Using WordPress on a server requires you to buy hosting and a domain name, whereas a WordPress.com website can use a sub-domain or an extension of a domain name like "mybiz.wordpress.com".

Some of the similarities in the two are (a) The ability to create and write blogs (b) The ability to add plugins (although the WordPress.com is limited) and (c) The ability to assign tags and categories to your blog posts. These similarities seem close to each other from the outset but there are more differences than similarities.

SEO or "Search Engine Optimization" was mentioned in an earlier blog. WordPress.org – is the serving station for a hosted website and provides the following: (a) The ability to add customized or corporate branded specialty themes, (b) connects with your domain name effortlessly and (c) allows you to create a robust website that does not resemble a blog. Your website looks just like a profession-al website, that also is a blog.

WordPress is the way to go no matter which version you choose. It is easy for the end user with little or no experience in website design, and no or little knowledge of how to create a website. WordPress websites enjoy natural and organic results on search engines such as Google because they have a very robust set of tagging and category options. Keep up with your writing and article creation using your blog, and you are well on your way to having loads of value content for your prospects. Order a Wordpress blog at www.lomancs.biz

A LANDING PAGE AND WEBSITE

A landing page is generally not something visitors will find through a search engine or stumble upon when browsing the internet. When people come to your landing page, it likely means they clicked on a specific link in an email you sent them or an ad you placed online. By clicking your link, the visitor has already expressed some interest in buying whatever it is your ad was focused on." Constant Contact, Jake Link, Senior Content Manager at Constant Contact.

THE MARKETING PLAN

I shared in the early chapters that I would share how branding culture plays a major role in marketing campaigns. It's true! You also need:

- PR plan
- Marketing Budget Planning
- Corporate Press Kit
- Press Release

In volume two of this book, l will cover what each of these means and why you need them.

Loman Creative Services
www.lomancreativeservices.com

Join e-newsletter at
www.marketingcampaignhandbook.com

Contact Bernice at
bernice@marketingcampaignhandbook.com to leave reviews and to acquire information about being a guest on the Marketing Campaign Handbook Podcast for entrepreneurs.
#marketingcampaignhandbook.com

LOMAN
CREATIVE
SERVICES

A ONE STOP SHOP FOR YOUR BRAND

TEXT LOMANCS TO 22828

Providing Excellent Services for Ministries & Businesses
Offering Additional Services With Our Trusted Partners
Offering Affordable Prices & Payment Plans

BRANDING
SOCIAL MEDIA
WEBSITE DESIGN
WEB HOSTING
WEB SECURITY
WEBSITE UPDATE
DOMAIN REGISTRATION
PROFESSIONAL EMAIL
EMAIL MARKETING

- CONTENT MARKETING
- CD & DVD DUPLICATION
- SEO
- VIDEOGRAPHY
- PHOTOGRAPHY
- TECHNOLOGY TRAINING
- GRAPHIC DESIGN
- ONLINE STORAGE

www.lomancreativeservices.com